Tell Me the Story

Written by
Max Lucado

Illustrations by
Ron DiCianni

Calligraphy by
Timothy R. Botts

CROSSWAY BOOKS • WHEATON, ILLINOIS
A DIVISION OF GOOD NEWS PUBLISHERS

ACKNOWLEDGMENTS

I am indebted to many for their contribution to this project as well as to my life. To Pastor Maddox for his research and input when it would have been easier to do what I felt like. To Lane, Jan and Mark for believing that a second Renaissance has been mandated in the halls of Heaven, then acting like it. To my wife Pat, my sons, Grant and Warren, who submitted to the call of God on my life, and like Abraham's family, stayed stride for stride with me even when they didn't know where we were going. Every painting has some of you three in it. To my mom for praying. To Max for listening. Finally to the Lord Jesus, the One and Only, who went by way of Calvary so that we could read it to our children.

—RON DiCIANNI

All credit for this project goes to the Author and Maker of life. I'm grateful to Ron DiCianni for the idea and vision, to the Crossway family for their dedication, and to my administrative assistant Karen Hill for incredible insight and skill.

—MAX LUCADO

Tell Me the Story.

Copyright © 1992 by Max Lucado.

Published by Crossway Books, a division of Good News Publishers,
1300 Crescent St., Wheaton, Illinois 60187.

Illustrations: Ron DiCianni

Calligraphy: Timothy R. Botts

Art Direction/Design: Mark Schramm

First printing, 1992

Printed in the United States of America

ISBN 0-89107-679-4

00	99	98	97	96	95	94	93	92
15	14	13	12	11	10	9 8	7 6	5 4	3 2	1

*Dedicated to
our dear friends and co-workers
Bryan and Becky Gibbs and their four sons:
Bryan, Lucas, Benjamin, and Samuel
In gratitude for a decade of
devotion to Brazil.*

—MAX LUCADO

Introduction

TWO-YEAR-OLD SARA SITS ON MY LAP. We are watching a comedy on television about a guy who has a mouse in his room. He is asleep. He opens one eye and finds himself peering into the face of the rodent. The camera gets eye-level with the mouse, and suddenly the screen is filled with two eyes, whiskers, and a twitching nose.

I laugh, but Sara panics. She turns away from the screen and buries her face in my shoulder. Her arms encircle my neck and clamp like a vise. Her little body grows rigid. She thinks the mouse is going to get her.

"It's ok, Sara," I assure her.

She won't let go. "It's only a picture."

She peers up at me with one eye and then burrows her nose back into my shirt.

"Mouse get me," she whimpers.

"There's nothing to be afraid of," I say. "It's only a pretend mouse."

I speak with confidence because I am confident. There is really nothing to fear. I know. I've seen big mice on picture screens before. I know they go away.

Sara doesn't. Two-year-olds don't understand the concept of television. As far as she knows, the rodent on the screen is about to bound out of the box and gobble her up. As far as she knows, the mouse will be there every time she comes into this room. As far as she knows, television sets are nothing more than glass cages that house giant mice. There *is* reason to be afraid.

So she is afraid.

But with time, I convince her. With time, she believes that the mouse is just a toy and that the tube can be turned off. Soon she relaxes on my lap, and we giggle at the man as his water faucet breaks and sprays him with water. Sara has gone from white-faced fear to peaceful chuckles in a few moments. Why? Because her father spoke and she believed.

Would that we would do the same. Got any giant mice on your screen? Got any fears that won't go away? Got any whiskered monsters staring at you?

I wish the fears were just television images. They aren't. They lurk in hospital rooms and funeral homes. They stare at us from divorce papers and eviction notices. They glare through the eyes of cruel parents or an abusive mate.

And we, like Sara, get frightened. But we, unlike Sara, don't know where to turn. Why did Sara turn to her dad for comfort? Simple. She knows me. Her world is comprised of a handful of people and I'm one of them. And it just so happens that I'm the biggest person in her world.

She thinks I'm strong. (I can pick her up!)

She thinks I'm smart. (I can drive a car.)

And she thinks I'm wise. (Please don't tell her the truth.)

And because she knows me, she trusts me. Instinctively, she is aware that I know more than she. So when I tell her not to worry, she doesn't worry.

Instinctively, we should know that God knows more than we do. Common sense would tell us that He isn't afraid of the mice that roar in our world.

We squirm at death. (He doesn't.)

We are afraid of tomorrows. (He isn't.)

We grow nervous in changing times. (Not God.)

He's been there before. He knows how these shows end. He knows that the worst fear the foe can throw is only a mirage. And He wants us to listen to His voice and trust Him—as Sara trusted me. To do that, however, we must do what Sara did. We must know our Father. And that is the goal Ron and I have in this book—to help you know your Father—

To help you know the Father who

     put the ocean in the palm of His hand,

          used His fingers to measure the sky,

               used scales to weigh the mountains.

And even more to help you know the Father who "takes care of His people like a shepherd," and "gathers them like lambs in His arms." These stories and paintings are for children from six to sixty who desire to see God.

There are times when mice roar. There are times when we need a strong pair of arms. You need to know that the arms of God are there.

It's up to you to turn to Him.

In the Beginning

In the beginning
God created the heavens
and the earth.

GENESIS 1:1 NIV

THE FATHER WAS DREAMING. I could see it in His eyes—the sparkle. It was there again.

"What is it You see, my King?"

He didn't turn, but kept His gaze fixed on the great emptiness—the massive, boundless, unending space. The more He looked, the more His eyes would dance. I knew He saw something.

I looked in the same direction. I leaned forward and stared intently. All I saw was emptiness. All I ever saw was emptiness.

I hadn't seen the sphere that He had pulled out of the sky. "Where was that?" I asked as He began molding it in His hands.

"It was there," He replied, looking outward. I looked and saw nothing. When I turned, He was smiling. He knew a seraph's vision was too limited.

The same thing happened with the water. "Where did this come from?" I asked, touching the strange substance.

"I saw it, Michael." He chuckled as He filled an ocean from His palm. "And when I saw it, I made it. I saw it near the stars."

"The what?"

"The stars." Out into the void He reached. When He pulled back His hand, He kept it closed as if to entice me to lean forward. I did. And just as my face was near, He opened His hand. A burst of light escaped, and I looked up just in time to see it illuminate His face, too. Once again, He was smiling.

"Watch how they sparkle," He reveled. And with a flip of His wrist, the palmful of diamonds soared into the blackness until they found their destiny, and there they hung.

"Won't the children love them?" the Maker said as together we watched the twinkling begin.

I still wasn't sure what or who these "children" were, but I knew they occupied a place in the Dream like nothing else. Ever since the Dream started, the Father spoke often of these children—what they would like, how they would respond.

I remember once, the Father held the sphere in one hand and motioned to me with the other. "Come. See what the children will see." He then put His fingers to His lips and blew gently. Off His fingertips floated tiny whiffs of white cotton balls of fluff.

"What do they do?" I asked as the train of puffs sailed toward the globe.

"Oh, Michael," He boomed with excitement, "they do everything. They give shade. They give rain. But most of all, My children can watch them pass and, if they look closely, they will see Me."

That was the way He thought about everything. All the Dream was for the children. And in all the Dream was the Father. With a waterfall, He said, "I made it small so they could run in and out." With the dandelion: "This is just the right size for the children to blow," and the rivers in the canyon: "They can sit right here and watch the water race into the valley."

"But where are the children?" I once asked, looking into the same space from whence had come the rest of the Dream.

"Oh, not out there," responded the Artist. There was urgency in His voice as He repeated, "Not out there."

But that is all the Father said. And that's all I asked.

With the coming of the creatures, I almost forgot. We laughed so much as

He made them. Each one was special. The tiny wing for the mosquito. The honk so unlike any other sound for the goose. The shell for the turtle. The darting eyes of the owl.

He even let me decorate a few. I put violet in the butterfly wings, and He loved my idea to stretch the elephant's nose.

What fun it was as the heavens gave birth to fowl and fish, reptile and rodent! No more had the little ones scurried off His palm than the giant ones appeared. He grabbed the giraffe and stretched its neck, and He put a hole in the whale's head ("so it will come to the surface to breathe and the children will see it").

"What will we call them all?" I asked.

"I'll leave that up to the children."

The children—I'd almost forgotten. But He hadn't. As the last winged creature left His fingers, He turned and looked at me and I knew.

"It's time?"

"Yes, it's time."

I expected to see His eyes dance again. But they didn't. I anticipated eagerness. But He didn't begin. For a long period, He sat looking out into the void—longer than normal.

"Do You see the children?"

"No. They are not to be found out there."

"Then what do You see?"

"I see their deeds."

He spoke softly. The joy was gone from His voice.

"What? What is it? What is it You see?"

Perhaps it was because He thought I needed to know. Or maybe because He needed someone else to know. I'm not sure why, but He did what He had never done. He let me see. As if the sky were a curtain, He took it and pulled it back.

Before I could see it, I could smell it. The stench stung my eyes. "It's greed you smell," He explained. "A love for foolish, empty things."

I started to turn away. But my King didn't, so I didn't. I looked again.

It was so dark—a darkness unlike the starless sky—a blackness unlike the void. This darkness moved. It crept. It shadowed and swayed. It was a living soot. He knew my thoughts and spoke.

His words were slow and spaced. "They will put it out."

"What?"

"They will destroy that which makes them Mine."

It was then I saw it for the first time. He reached into Himself—deep into His own self and pulled it out. A flame. A shining circle.

It glowed brilliantly in His palm. Much brighter than the constellations He had spread about or the sun He'd ignited.

"This is . . . " I began.

"This is a part of Me," He finished and added what I couldn't have imagined. "And out of Me, I will make My children."

For the first time I saw. I saw why the children were so treasured. I saw the uniqueness in them. They bore His light—the universe He created, the children He fathered.

"But the darkness?" I had to ask. "Why?"

"Just as I chose, so must they choose. Else they won't be Mine."

Just then His face lifted. His eyes brightened. "But they won't all forget Me. Look."

Into tomorrow I gazed. At first I saw nothing. Just swarthy darkness billowing. But then, as I searched, I saw. First, only one, then a cluster, then more—lights they were. Flickers of candles, weakened but not lost in the blackness. Like the stars He had cast against the black heavens, these flames flickered in a sable sea.

"It's My children." There was pride in His voice. "My children remember."

The look on His face, I cannot forget. His eyes had sparkled when He suspended the planets in space; His cheeks had danced as He heard the cat purr. I had seen His face alive before—but not like now. For at this moment—when He saw His children alight in the darkness—when He saw those who were His seeking Him—He celebrated. His countenance exploded with joy. His head flew back, and laughter shook the stars.

"My children, My children, My children," were His only words. And then, He paused, wiped the tears from His face, and pledged a promise for all of Heaven to hear.

"You haven't forgotten Me; I won't forget you."

Then He turned to me. "To the work, Michael; we've much to do. We must make the Dream come true."

And I thought making the animals was a delight. "No two will be alike," He vowed as He began reaching into Himself for balls of light. "Some big, some small. Some timid, some bold. Some with big ears, some with little." And off His palm they came. Generation chosen. Destination determined. Each with a different thread of character or shape of body.

But each with a bit of Him—a light within.

And He even let me help. "Look what I made, Father," I told him. "I call them freckles. Let me show You how they work."

And He smiled.

The Fall

You may eat from the fruit of any
tree in the garden, but you must not eat
the fruit from the tree which gives
the knowledge of good and evil. If you
ever eat fruit from that tree,
you will die!

GENESIS 2:17

LONG AGO IN A LAND FAR AWAY and unlike any you've ever seen, there lived a wise man named Shaddai. Shaddai was a large man with a tender heart. He had bright blue eyes and a long, thick beard. When He laughed, which is something He did often, His cheeks would lift until His eyes became half-moons of joy.

When He sang, which is something else He did often, everything stopped to listen. Tall aspens would bend. Squirrels, butterflies, and birds would pause. Even the children would turn when they heard His voice. And well they should. It was for them He sang.

And for them He built a wonderful village. It was more than any child could dream. The children plunged into the pond fed by the underwater spring. They shrieked as they soared high on the long swings under the thick-branched apple trees. They scampered through the grass-carpeted meadows and fruit-filled

orchards. The sun never seemed to set too early, and the night sky always soothed. And, most of all, Shaddai was always near.

When Shaddai wasn't in the meadow with the children or in the orchards with the children, He was in the workshop—with the children. They loved to smell the sawdust, hear Him sing, and watch Him carve a chair out of a log or make a table out of a tree. They would gather around Him and take turns laying their tiny hands flat against His huge one.

Every night He would gather the children on the grassy meadow and tell them stories. Spellbound, the children would listen as long as Shaddai—or their weary eyes—allowed.

The children loved Shaddai. And Shaddai loved the children. When they called His name, He dropped whatever He was doing and turned. His giant heart had a hundred strings—each held by a different child.

That's why He built the wall.

The wall was a stone fence surrounding the village. With great care Shaddai had laid each rock upon the other. The base of the fence was wider than two of His strides. The wall rose above Shaddai, even with His hand stretched skyward. He spent days building the fence. And as He built, He did not sing.

A deadly wilderness lay outside the village. As Shaddai built the fence, He would often pause and look into its shadows. Cruel thorns and savage beasts and hidden pits filled the dark forest. It was no place for children with soft skin. Certain death awaited any who would enter.

"Beyond the wall is no life," He would tell the children in solemn tones. "You were made for My village, not for the terrible land beyond. Stay with Me. It's safe here."

But in His heart He knew it was only a matter of time.

The day He placed the final stone on the wall, He returned to His shop, took a long aspen branch and carved a staff, and stood it in a corner. He would be ready.

One day a boy ran into Shaddai's workshop. The sandy-haired child with searching eyes and restless energy brought the Maker both joy and concern.

"Shaddai!"

In one motion the Builder dropped His hammer and turned. "What is it, Paladin?"

The boy spoke in spurts as he gasped for air. "The wall . . . I found an . . .

opening. It's a large opening, Sire." The boy's hands stretched to show the size. "Someone could crawl through it."

Shaddai pulled over a stool and sat down. "I knew it would be you, Paladin, my child. Tell me, how did you find it?"

"I was walking along the wall searching for—"

"Holes?"

Paladin paused, surprised that Shaddai knew. "Yes, I was looking for holes."

"So you could see out into the forest?"

"I was curious, Shaddai. I wanted to know what is so bad out there that You won't let us go."

Shaddai motioned for the boy to come. When he got close, the Maker cupped the small face in His hands and lifted it so the boy would look directly into His eyes. The urgency of the look caused Paladin's stomach to feel hollow.

"Paladin, listen to Me. The regions beyond are not for you. They are not for Me. A journey into the wilderness will bring death. You were not made for those lands. Let your feet carry you to the many places you can go—not to the one place you can't. If you leave here, you will not find the way back."

Paladin spoke softly. "You will fix the hole then?"

"No, Paladin, I created it."

"You broke the wall? But You just said You didn't want us to leave."

"I don't want you to leave. But I left the opening when I built the wall."

"But unless You fix it—"

"—the children might leave. I know, Paladin. But as long as the children have to stay, they aren't really here."

Paladin didn't understand, but he didn't want to ask any more questions. Uncomfortable, he turned to leave. As he entered the sunlight, he looked back into the shop. There sat Shaddai, leaning forward, still looking at Paladin.

Paladin was confused. Part of him wanted the safety of Shaddai's shop, while another part drew him toward the fence. He looked again into the shop. Shaddai was standing now—not moving, but standing. His large hand stretched out to the boy.

Paladin turned quickly away, as if not to see. He walked as fast as he could, aimlessly at first, then purposely toward the fence.

"I won't get too near," he said to himself. "I'll just peek out."

Questions came as quickly as his steps. *What is this pull I feel . . . this curiosity? Why would Shaddai tell me to deny an urge I feel so strongly? Is a desire to see beyond the fence so wrong?*

By now he was at the hole. Without stopping to think, he lay on his stomach and squirmed through just far enough to stick his head out the other side.

"Why would a journey there bring death?" Paladin asked himself as he peered at the forbidden forest. "What is it that Shaddai is protecting me from or . . . keeping me from?"

As if his knees were moving on their own, Paladin crept further. Soon his body was through the hole, and he rose slowly to his feet. For several moments he didn't move. He wondered if something would come out of the trees to hurt him. Nothing did. He relaxed his shoulders and sighed. "It's not so bad," he spoke aloud to break the silence. "It's nice out here. What was Shaddai worried about?"

Paladin began walking into the forest. Twigs snapped beneath his bare feet. Sweet flowers scented the air. The trees were so thick he could barely see the sky. "Just a few steps into the woods," he spoke aloud though no one could hear. "To see what it's like."

After a dozen more steps he stopped. He liked the wilderness. "Nothing to fear here." For the first time in his young life, he believed that Shaddai was wrong. "Just wait until I tell the others." And he turned to go back through the hole.

But the hole was gone!

He stopped and stared. He saw only solid wall. Paladin ran to the fence and stooped at the very spot where he'd come through. He knew this was the place. But there was no hole and no sign that there had ever been one. He ran a dozen steps one way and then a dozen steps the other. Nothing.

Suddenly he heard a strange sound in the woods behind him. He swung around, but he saw nothing. Paladin looked into the forest. Now it no longer seemed friendly. It was dark and threatening, as if it were about to devour him.

Desperately, Paladin searched the fence. It was too tall to climb over, too thick to break through. There was no way home.

"If you leave here, you will not find the way back." Shaddai's words rang in his mind.

The boy's eyes were wide with fear. He sat on the ground and hugged his knees to his chest and began to cry.

"Shaddai, Shaddai! I'm so sorry. Please come help me."

Paladin's plea had been heard before he spoke it. For as he left Shaddai's workshop, the Maker had watched him as long as He could. When the boy was out of sight, Shaddai turned, not to take up His work but to remove His apron. He hung His tools on the wall. Then He reached into the corner and took the staff, the one He'd carved after He finished the fence.

Even before Paladin had reached the fence, Shaddai had left the shop. Even before Paladin had asked for help, Shaddai was on the way to give it. Even before the hole in the fence had closed, Shaddai had opened another. His strong hands pulled away the rocks until He could see into the forest.

With His staff at His side, Shaddai crawled through the hole. He left the village He'd made and entered the land for which He wasn't made and set out in search of His child.

Resurrection Morning

He is not here.
He has risen from the dead
as he said he would.

MATTHEW 28:6

ELL IT AGAIN, YOU SAY? Tell it again? I've told you all I know. I've even told you what I don't know."

"But some are just arriving. They haven't heard what you saw. Tell us again."

The heavy door opened and shut quickly as two more men entered the small room. Claudius supposed this was a storage room, but he wasn't sure. It was too dark. The only light was a slit of afternoon sunshine creeping through an opening in the wooden shutters and streaking across the faces of the listeners.

The group numbered fifteen, maybe twenty—about as many men as women. A few men were shaven, most bearded. A few asked questions. A few shook their heads. All sat with eyes fixed on the young soldier whose story they longed to hear but didn't know whether to believe.

Claudius took a breath and began his story again. "I wasn't supposed to work that night. I'd worked over the Sabbath and was tired. In fact, I had been on duty since Friday morning."

"I remember your face." The voice belonged to a woman sitting on the floor. "You were on the hill."

"I was assigned the Golgotha detail a month ago." A grumble went up from the group. Claudius defended himself. "I didn't ask for it. I was given it."

Emotion was thick in the room, but then someone was urging, "Go on, finish the story!"

Claudius again shifted his weight. He would never have imagined himself in a room full of Jews. The contrast between his trimmed hair and short uniform and their beards and robes only added to his discomfort. He eyed his spear on the floor at his feet. His Roman shield leaned against the adobe wall. Coming here was a dangerous move.

He had been uneasy ever since he had arrived in Jerusalem a few months back. Certainly wasn't his choice of a place to serve, but when Rome sends, a soldier obeys. Besides, he told himself, a year in a peaceful outpost couldn't be too bad.

Wrong. Jerusalem was far from peaceful. The Jews hated the soldiers. The soldiers distrusted the Jews. If it wasn't the priests' complaints, it was the zealots' riots. Forget casual strolls down the street keeping the peace. Jerusalem was a hotbed of anger. Anger at Rome. Anger at the world.

They called themselves the people of God. Some nation of God! No navy. Puny army. No emperor. Just a Temple, a Torah, and some strange rules about the Sabbath. Claudius had been trained to respect strength and size—neither of which he found here.

Until last night. What he saw last night he'd never seen in Rome or anywhere else. When he told his officers about it, they told him to keep quiet. He couldn't. He had to have some answers. So he came here. These people wanted answers, too. So they let him in.

They were easy to find. Every soldier in the city knew where they were hiding—the upper room of the large white corner house. It was the same place they had met last week when He was still here.

One by one they had drifted back to the room—each entering with a knock on the door and a shameful nod. When Claudius learned how they had run away and left Him alone, he was amazed that they had returned. "Why are you still here then?" he had asked. "Why don't you go home?"

"If you'd seen Him do what we've seen Him do, you would stay, too," a disciple explained.

"Sounds like he has," added another.

For by now they all knew what had happened at the tomb. Or better, they knew something had happened at the tomb. No one quite knew how to explain it. Claudius picked up his story where he'd left off.

"When I first saw Him being led up the hill, I noticed He was different. He didn't demand we let Him go. He didn't shout or resist. And when we hammered the spike into His hand—" Claudius paused, wondering if he should have mentioned this. An encouraging nod from one of the women told him to continue. "—when we placed the spike in His hand, He held His hand still. He didn't fight."

"Sounds like something He would do," a man in the back stated. Several nodded in agreement.

"He never seemed angry." Claudius's voice grew softer as he continued. "He never blamed anyone. People were cursing and laughing at Him, but not once did I see His eyes lose their calm."

No one moved as Claudius spoke. When he had shared these events with his superiors earlier in the day, they had scoffed. It didn't matter to the Romans how Jesus had acted. But it mattered to these people. They wanted to know every detail. For the first time Claudius felt a camaraderie with his listeners—a camaraderie based on a fascination with one Man.

He continued, "'Forgive them,' I heard Him say. And when He spoke, I looked up. He was looking at me. His face was a mask of blood and spit. But He was praying for me."

The only movement in the room was the nodding of heads.

"After the crucifixion I helped lower the body and lay it on the ground. I waited as these women—" He motioned to several near the front. "I waited as they prepared the body, and then I saw that it was placed in the tomb.

"I thought my day was over. It took four men to close the grave's opening with a huge stone. When we turned to leave, word came that Pilate and the Temple leaders were nervous that someone would steal the body. We were told to seal the tomb and stand guard all night.

"There were several of us, so we built a fire and took turns. I was the first to sleep. When they woke me for my turn, it was an hour before dawn. The night was black—as black as any night I can remember. The moon was small, and the stars were hidden by the clouds.

"I stood on one side. Another soldier stood on the other. He laughed about how easy it was to guard a tomb. Not often does a soldier get guard duty in a cemetery. Maybe we dozed off, because at first I thought I was dreaming. The ground began to shake—violently. It shook so hard I fell to the ground. Rocks fell from the walls behind us. Sparks flew from the fire. The soldiers asleep on the ground jumped up. I know they were standing because when the light hit them, I could see their faces like it was broad daylight."

"What light?" someone asked.

"You tell me!" Claudius demanded. "Where did that light come from? The rock rolled back and the light roared out. A burst of fire with no heat. A gust of wind blew from the tomb, put out the fire, knocked us back, and the next thing I knew, the tomb was empty. I looked at the soldiers. They were stunned. About that time these two women appeared."

"That's when we saw the angel!" Mary blurted. "He was sitting on the rock! He told us that Jesus was not here. He told us that . . ."

She hesitated, knowing her words would be hard to believe.

"He told us that Jesus is no longer dead!"

Her words rang in the room like the peal of a bell. No one dared speak. Finally one did. A clean-shaven younger man said softly, but firmly, "Just like He said he would."

"You mean, He said He would do this?" Claudius asked.

"More than once. But we didn't understand. We didn't believe. Until today."

"John," one of the women asked the man speaking, "you were there. You went to the tomb. Is that what you saw?"

"Peter and I saw the tomb. We saw it open and empty. But we didn't see Jesus."

Once again the room was quiet. Then Claudius broke the silence. "I have a question. I've told you what you wanted to know. Now you tell me what I want to know. This has been on my mind all weekend. It's been on my heart ever since I struck the nail into Jesus' hand. Who is this man? Who is this Jesus?"

If any head had hung before, it lifted at this moment. If any thoughts had wandered, they wandered no more.

"Is there any doubt?" Mary said. Her eyes were bright. She jumped to her feet as she spoke. "I saw Him! I saw Him risen from the dead. He is who He said He was. He is the Son of God!"

With that statement the room broke into chaos.

"Impossible!"

"No, she is right. Let her speak!"

"Why did He let them kill Him if He is the Son of God?"

"It doesn't make sense."

"What doesn't make sense is why you can't believe!"

Claudius was silent. What he was hearing, he could not handle. But what he had seen at the grave, he could not deny. He leaned over and put his elbows on his knees and buried his face in his hands. Thoughts rumbled in his head. He was so intent that he didn't notice the sudden silence. Stillness reigned for several seconds before he raised his head. A light filled the room. He looked at the door and the window; they were still closed.

Faces that had been cast in shadows now beamed. All eyes stared in his direction—not at him, but behind him. But before he could turn to see what they were seeing, a hand was on his shoulder. When Claudius turned to looked at the hand, he found the answer for his heart.

The hand was pierced.

Into His Presence

Blessed are the pure in heart,
for they will see God.

MATTHEW 5:8 NIV

A LONG TIME AGO in a land much like your own, there was a village. And in this village lived five orphans. A lonely family of fatherless children, they had banded together against the cold. One day a king learned of their misfortune and decided to adopt them. He decreed that he would be their father and planned to come for them.

All the people in the land thought it odd that the king should adopt these children. He already had many people to care for.

"Why does the king want them?" the people would ask. But the king had his reasons.

When the children learned that they had a new father, and their father was *the king* (no less!), and the king was coming to visit, they went wild with excitement.

When the people of the village learned that the children had a father, and their father was *the king*, and that the king was coming to the village, they were terribly excited as well. They went out to see the children and told them what to do.

"You need to impress the king," they explained. "Only those with great gifts to give will be allowed to live in the castle."

The people didn't know the king. They just assumed that all kings want to be impressed. So the children worked long and hard preparing their offerings. One boy, who knew how to carve, determined to give the king a wonderful work of wooden art. He set his knife against the soft skin of the elm and whittled. The small blocks of wood came alive with the eyes of a sparrow or the nose of a unicorn.

His sister decided to present the king with a painting that captured the beauty of the heavens—a painting worthy to hang in his castle.

Another sister chose music as her way to impress the king. For long hours she practiced with her voice and mandolin. Village people would stop at her window and listen as her music took wings and soared.

Yet another child set out to turn the king's head with his wisdom. Late hours would find his candle lit and his books open. Geography. Mathematics. Chemistry. The breadth of his study was matched only by the depth of his desire. Surely a sage such as the king would appreciate all his hard work.

But there was one little girl who had nothing to offer. Her hand was clumsy with the knife, her fingers stiff with the brush. She opened her mouth to sing, but the sound was hoarse. She was too dull to read. She had no talent. She had no gift.

All she had to offer was her heart, for her heart was good. She spent her time at the city gates, watching the people come and go. She would make pennies by grooming their horses or feeding their animals. A stable girl she was—a stable girl with no stable. But she had a good heart.

She knew the beggars by name. She took time to pet each dog. She welcomed home the travelers and greeted the strangers.

"How was the journey?" she would ask.

"Tell me what you learned on your visit."

"How is your husband?"

"Do you enjoy your new work?"

She was full of questions for people because her heart was big and she cared about people. But since she had no talent and no gift, she grew anxious that the king would be angry. The villagers told her that the king would want a gift and that she should set her mind about the task of making one. So she took a small knife and went to her brother, the carver.

"Could you teach me to carve?" she asked.

"Sorry," the young crafter responded without looking up. "I've much work to do. I haven't time for you. The king is coming, you know."

The girl put away her knife and picked up a brush. She went to her sister, the artist. She found her on a hill painting a sunset on a canvas.

"You paint so well," said the girl who had no gift but a big heart.

"I know," the painter answered.

"Could you share with me your gift?"

"Not now," the sister responded with eyes on her palette. "The king is coming, you know."

The girl with no gift then remembered her other sister, the one with the song. "She will help me," she said. But when she arrived at her sister's house, she found a crowd of people waiting to listen to her sister sing.

"Sister," she called, "sister, I've come to listen and learn." But her sister couldn't hear. The noise of the applause was too loud.

Heart heavy, the girl turned and walked away. Then she remembered her other brother. She took a book with small words and big letters and went to see him. "I have nothing to offer the king," she said. "Could you teach me to read so I might show him my wisdom?"

The young sage-to-be didn't speak. He was lost in thought. The child with no gift spoke again. "Could you help me? I have no talent—"

"Go away," said the scholar, scarcely moving his eyes from the text. "Can't you see I'm preparing myself for the coming of the king?"

And so the girl went away sorrowfully. She had nothing to give. She returned to her place at the city gates and took up her task of caring for people's animals.

After some days a man in merchant's dress came to the small town.

"Can you feed my donkey?" he asked the girl. The orphan jumped to her feet and looked into the brown face of the one who had traveled far. His skin was leathery from the sun, and his eyes were deep. A kind smile from beneath the beard warmed the girl.

"That I can," the girl answered and eagerly took the animal to the trough. "Trust him with me. When you return, he will be groomed and fed."

"Tell me," she asked as the donkey drank, "have you come to stay?"

"For only a while."

"Are you weary from your journey?"

"That I am."

"Would you like to sit and rest?" The girl motioned to a bench near the wall. The tall man with the dark skin sat on the bench, leaned against the wall, closed his eyes, and slept. After a few minutes he opened them and found the girl sitting at his feet, looking at his face. She was embarrassed that he had caught her staring. She turned away.

"Have you sat there long?"

"Yes."

"What do you seek?"

"Nothing. You seem to be a kind man with a peaceful heart. It's good to be near you."

The man smiled and stroked his beard. "You are a wise girl," he said. "When I return, we will visit more."

The man did return—quite soon.

"Did you find whom you sought?" the girl asked.

"I found them, but they were too busy for me."

"What do you mean?"

"Those I came to see were too busy to see me. One was a woodsmith rushing to complete a project. He told me to return tomorrow. Another was an artist. I saw her sitting on a hillside, but the people below said she did not want to be disturbed. The other was a musician. I sat with the others and listened to her music. When I asked to talk with her, she said she had no time. The other I sought had left. He has moved to the city to go to school."

The girl's eyes widened.

"But you don't look like a king," she gasped.

"I try not to," he explained. "Being a king can be lonely. People act strangely around me. They ask for favors. They try to impress me. They bring me all their complaints."

"But isn't that what a king is for?" asked the girl.

"Certainly," responded the king, "but there are times when I just want to be with my people. There are times when I want to talk to my people—to hear about their day, to laugh a bit, to cry some. There are times when I just want to be their father."

"Is that why you adopted the children?"

"That's why. Children like to talk. Adults think they have to impress me; children don't. They just want to talk to me."

"But my brothers and sisters were too busy?"

"They were. But I'll come back. Maybe they'll have more time another day. Would you like to ride on my donkey to the castle?"

And so it happened that the children with many talents but no time missed the visit of the king, while the girl whose only gift was her time to talk became his child.

Spiritual Warfare

You only need to remain calm;
the Lord will fight for you.

EXODUS 14:14

JOHN COLE KNEW SOMETHING WAS WRONG the moment he walked into the house. It was quiet—too quiet.

"Honey?" he called.

"Andrea? Jeff? Anyone home?"

"Up here, John."

John climbed the stairs. He found his son and wife in Jeff's room, the boy face down on the bed, crying into the pillow. Andrea was sitting at his side.

John didn't say anything. He sat on the side of the bed and put his hand on Jeff's back. After a moment he looked up at Andrea. "The Bryan boys again?"

She spoke slowly, trying to control her anger. "They were waiting for him after school. When he came out, the oldest one, Bobby, was sitting on Jeff's bike, and the other brothers were blocking Jeff's way. When Jeff asked for his bike back, one of the boys pushed him down."

"Did they hit him?"

"No, but they said they would if I didn't give them a dollar," said Jeff, looking at his father, his face wet with tears. "It's not right what they did, Dad. It's not right."

"I know, son, I know." John cupped Jeff's face in his hands and rubbed away the tears. "We'll talk more after dinner."

✧✧✧

Jeff could not see the two visitors who entered his room while he rested. He could not hear the flurry of their wings—or their conversation.

"What could they want with this little fellow?" It was Paragon who spoke first. "He has harmed no one."

"They lurk around the young, Paragon. And they find evil hearts to do their bidding," replied Aegis, his companion.

The strength of the two angels filled the room—wide shoulders rounded with muscles, strong arms folded, swords ready in their belts, faces firm and solemn. Their soft white robes glowed. And their eyes were filled with anger.

✧✧✧

After dinner John had an idea. "Let's go into the living room," he suggested. "I've got something to show you."

When the three were seated on the couch, John reached over to the coffee table and picked up the large family Bible. He opened it carefully to one of the color plates. It was a picture Jeff had looked at many times—Moses standing near the edge of a big sea, the sky behind him black with clouds, his hair and robe blown back by the wind. An army of chariots raced toward him from one side, and a large group of people stood in front of him. The soldiers in the chariots looked mean, and the people looked afraid, but Moses seemed calm. He was holding up his staff and facing the heavens.

The words just below the picture read, "Remain calm. The Lord will fight for you."

"Who do you think said those words, son?" John asked.

"Moses?" Jeff guessed.

"You're right. Do you think he was afraid?"

"I would have been. With all those bad guys coming and all those people asking for help, I would have been afraid."

32

Andrea spoke up. "He's trapped. He has the sea on one side and the army on the other—where can he go?"

"That's how I felt today with the Bryan boys, Dad," said Jeff. "I felt trapped."

John closed the Bible and put it back on the table. "I know, son. That's why we have to do what Moses did. We have to ask God to take over."

✧✧✧

Paragon and Aegis stood behind the family looking at the picture.

"I don't remember Moses as being that tall," Paragon said.

"He wasn't," Aegis explained, "but the guy who painted the picture didn't know that."

"The rest looks right though. Remember when God sent us down to blow open the sea and let the people go through?"

"You bet I do. That was great. Looks like we'll be called to stir up a few more things pretty soon."

✧✧✧

It was almost midnight when John walked into his son's room. Jeff was asleep. Andrea was asleep in the other room. But John had spent almost an hour sitting on the couch with the open Bible on his lap, reading God's promises of help:

"I made you and will take care of you. I will carry you and save you."[1]

"The Lord searches all the earth for people who have given themselves completely to him. He wants to make them strong."[2]

"The angel of the Lord camps around those who fear God, and he saves them."[3]

"He has put his angels in charge of you to watch over you wherever you go."[4]

"Don't think these little children are worth nothing. I tell you they have angels in heaven who are always with my father in heaven."[5]

"Wow!" John said out loud. "Those are the words of Jesus!"

With each verse he could almost feel the power of God in the room. He set the open Bible on the table and walked quickly up the stairs, with Aegis and Paragon close behind. He knelt beside his son's bed and began to pray.

"Paragon, quick!" Aegis cried. "Look out the window."

In the blackness of the night sky shadowy black followers of the devil were coming toward Jeff's room. As the father prayed, the angels went into action. "Oh no you don't!" they cried at the same time. In an instant Paragon and Aegis were in the sky with wings spread and swords drawn.

"This boy is not yours to take!" Aegis declared.

Just the sound of the angels' voices made the black shadows flee.

"And don't come back, you turkeys!" yelled Paragon after them.

When Jeff awoke the next morning, he found a note from his dad on the pillow.

"Remember the words of Moses, Jeff, 'Remain calm. The Lord will fight for you.' I don't know how He will do it, son, but trust God and He will take care of you."

As Jeff rode his bike to school, he kept saying the words of Moses over and over, "Keep calm. The Lord will fight for you."

Jeff had just turned the first corner when he saw a barricade blocking the road, which was flooded with water.

"Funny," he said to himself, "I didn't hear it storm last night."

He turned his bike around and took another street to school. As he rounded the corner, he heard a crash and a thud. He looked up and saw a boy lying next to a parked car with his bicycle on its side, wheels still spinning.

Jeff raced to the fallen boy, who was groaning in pain. It was Billy Bryan—the youngest of the Bryan brothers! "I wasn't looking," Billy moaned. "I didn't see the car. I just rode right into it."

Billy was holding his elbow. When Jeff saw the blood, he knew what to do.

"Stay right here. I'll go get some help," he said. But when he turned, he ran right into the arms of a man. It was his dad!

"I was following you," he explained. "Just in case something happened."

The next few minutes were a blur of activity—Jeff telling his dad what had happened, John carrying Billy, Andrea bandaging Billy's arm.

That's when Billy realized where he was. He'd been crying so hard he hadn't even noticed who had helped him. "Wait a minute," he said, "you're Jeff Cole."

Jeff didn't speak.

"We took your bike yesterday." Jeff still said nothing. "But you helped me anyway." Billy's voice was soft with wonder.

Andrea smiled at Jeff. "Things will be better now."

John smiled at Andrea. "God did it again."

And above the group, Aegis smiled at Paragon. "That was a clever move—blowing that water across the road so Jeff would take a different road to school."

"I learned it at the Red Sea," Paragon chuckled. "I wonder if someday someone will paint a picture of Jeff helping Billy."

Aegis laughed. "If they do, I hope they don't make him look too tall."

---

[1]Isaiah 46:4;   [2]2 Chronicles 16:9;   [3]Psalm 34:7;   [4]Psalm 91:11;   [5]Matthew 18:10

The Prodigal

While the son was still a long way off,
his father saw him and felt sorry for his son.
So the father ran to him and hugged
and kissed him.

LUKE 15:20

WHY WERE THEY ALWAYS at each other's throats? Bill felt as if he hardly knew his son any longer. Josh was demanding the money his mother had left him when she died. That money was for college expenses, and Josh could only have it after he turned eighteen. Now he was eighteen, and he wanted it, but not for college.

"It's mine, isn't it?" he had shouted.

"Of course, it's yours," his father had replied. "But it's college money, not play money."

"I'm not going to play, Dad. I'm just going away."

"Where? For what?"

"I don't know. I just want to get out."

And so the arguments had gone on for weeks. It was only this morning that Bill had made his decision. Long before the sun came up, he went into Josh's room and sat beside the bed. He didn't know what time Josh had come in the night before,

but the smell of beer suggested it hadn't been early. Josh hadn't even undressed. He was sleeping in his jeans.

The father stared at his son's face for a long time. Years ago when he would come in from business trips, he would pull a chair up beside the bed of his sleeping boy. He'd push back the mop of hair from Josh's forehead and touch the soft cheeks. Everything seemed so simple then. The biggest challenge was airing up a bicycle tire or catching a fly ball. Now the boy's earring, the weird haircut, the tattoo . . . it was as if his son lived in a different world, a world the father could not understand—but feared.

"We lost something, Josh," he said to his sleeping son. "Maybe we never had it. Maybe we buried it with your mom." Bill's hand was again on the forehead of his son.

By the time Josh awoke, Bill knew what he had to do.

"I'll give you the money," he had told Josh at breakfast. "Get your things. I'll take you to the airport."

Now as they waited for the plane, Josh interrupted his thoughts.

"Dad, they're boarding."

The two walked toward the gate and stopped.

"I guess I've got everything," Josh said quietly as he turned to his father.

What Josh saw next he'd never seen before—and never expected. Tears. Though the father blinked and turned away as if to look out the window, Josh saw them.

Josh plopped on the floor beside the bucket. He looked at the clock on the wall. Three A.M. He was so tired. He'd cleaned the kitchen, washed the bathrooms, done several loads of laundry, and now he was mopping the bunkrooms.

He reached to take a cigarette out of his shirt pocket only to find the pocket empty. When you don't have money, you don't have cigarettes.

With his back against the wall and his arms resting on his knees, he looked into the semidarkness of the bunkroom. Though he couldn't see their faces, he could hear their snoring—a room full of drifters and drunks. Some were running away. Some were coming back. But all were dreaming of a better place. All were longing for home.

Of all the places Josh thought he would end up living, a Salvation Army bunkhouse wasn't one of them. When he had arrived in the city three months ago, he was cocky and rich. The only thing he flashed more than his money was his grin.

He bought a car. He rented an apartment. Got new clothes. He had more friends than he could count.

Then came the call from the bank. He was out of money. That night a restaurant refused his credit card. He couldn't make the payments on the car. The dealer took it back. He sold his stereo. He pawned his jewelry. Someone stole his backpack and his wallet. Every day the circle of friends got smaller. Finally he couldn't pay the rent. They kicked him out.

Josh spent the next week on the streets—the same streets where he had turned heads with his style. He now turned heads because of his stink. That's when he heard about this shelter where you could sleep in exchange for ten hours of work.

"Hard to believe I've been in this place for a month," Josh said to himself as he sat on the floor. "A month of dishes and trash cans and cleaning up the vomit of people too drunk to make it to the bathroom."

For just a moment he allowed his thoughts to drift homeward. Memories of a warm bed. Good meals. Conversations on the porch. He thought of the farm. He thought of his father's workmen coming in at the end of the week to collect their pay.

"Those guys have it better than I do," he sighed. "Even the guy who cuts Dad's grass has a good meal and a home."

Funny. Just a few months ago home was a prison with too many rules—a cage holding a bird who wanted to be free. But now Josh was longing for home.

He stood and took a few steps into the bunkroom he was about to clean. Suddenly he saw his face in the mirror. It looked different. He pushed back his hair and stared at his reflection. He saw something he'd never seen before. He saw his dad. He'd been told he looked like his father—but he couldn't see it. Tonight he did. Same chin. Same nose.

"Dad." In his mind he saw his father again. In the airport his father's words hadn't come, but his tears had. And the tears had said more than any words ever could have.

Josh stood straight up and spoke aloud—so loud that the guy in the nearest bunk rolled over. Josh didn't care.

"I'm going home."

He put down the mop and the bucket and walked out into the night.

Hank sips the coffee in the styrofoam cup and sets it back on the dash. This is his favorite time of the day—early morning just as the gray sky gives way to gold. Like most truck drivers, he drives at night. But, unlike other drivers, Hank likes to stay on the road a few hours into the morning.

"Every sunrise is a miracle," he'd tell them as he would leave the truck stop. "Who wants to miss a miracle?"

In his thirty years on the road Hank had seen many sunrises, most of them alone. This morning, however, he is about to have company. As he turns his truck onto the highway, he sees a hitchhiker—a young man in jeans and a tattered shirt.

Hank doesn't often pick up riders. But something about the boy catches his eye. He pulls his rig over to the side of the road. In his side mirror he can see the boy running toward him. Hank leans over and opens the passenger door.

"Thanks for stopping." The hitchhiker is nearly out of breath. "Going far?"

"At least another two hours south."

"That's all I need." The young man climbs into the truck.

"Where you headed?" Hank inquires.

"Home."

"Been gone long?"

When the boy turns to answer, Hank hears sorrow in his voice. "Too long, sir. Too long."

"My name's Hank."

"Josh is mine," responds the boy.

Hank looks at Josh's dirty clothes and weary eyes. "Looks like you could use a good night's rest and a meal."

"Yeah. I've kind of hit hard times." Before he knows it, Josh finds himself telling his story.

When he finishes, he looks up into Hank's eyes, which are warm with compassion.

"So you finally got so hungry you decided to go home?"

Josh pauses a moment before he answers. "No, it wasn't that. I mean, I could have handled the job. I might have even gotten on my feet."

"Then what made you decide to go home, Josh?"

"The thought of what I did to my dad. I broke his heart. I need to tell him I'm sorry."

"Are you going to stay home?"

"I don't know, Hank. I'm going to see if I might get work nearby. But I don't think Dad will want me under the same roof . . . Whoa," he says suddenly, "this is where I get off."

Hank doesn't slow down. "No need, son. I'll take you right to your door." Hank guides the semi down the exit and onto the small road. Following Josh's instructions, he weaves in and out of the farms and flatlands.

Hank notices that Josh isn't saying much. The boy is staring at the floor of the truck. His hands are clenched between his knees. The seasoned driver places his hand on the boy's shoulder. "Josh, it's going to be—"

"What if he doesn't even let me in the gate?" Josh interrupts. "What if he doesn't let me tell what happened?"

"Josh, I'm a dad. I know how dads feel. You've got to tell your father the truth. Give him a chance to forgive you."

Josh looks over at the driver and then watches his father's fields come into view. "We're almost there."

When they reach the house, Hank pulls the rig over to the side of the narrow road and stops.

"I'll wait here." He smiles. "Just tell him the truth, Josh."

Josh nods, takes a breath, and opens the door. "Thanks for the ride and thanks for the advice."

Hank watches as the tall boy walks slowly down the path toward the house. Hank can tell that Josh is talking as he walks. He is rehearsing what he is going to say.

He is only halfway to the house when at the top of the trail a figure appears. Though Hank has never seen him, he knows in an instant it is Josh's father. Only a dad would do what this man is doing. Running. Running fast. Arms spread wide and a smile no one can miss. For a few moments Hank doesn't speak. He just memorizes the scene of the morning sun rising behind the dejected boy and the running father.

Finally Hank can stand it no longer. "Josh," he yells, "look!"

When Josh sees his father only feet away and getting closer, he falls to his knees. He tries to speak, but once again the words won't come. His well-rehearsed speech is forgotten as he throws his arms around his father's waist.

Hank wipes away tears of his own as he starts his truck. He has seen what he came to see. He has seen the miracle of the morning.

Before It's Too Late

It will be the same when the Son of Man
comes. Two men will be in the field. One will
be taken and the other will be left.

MATTHEW 25:41

THE TWO BOYS LOOKED AT THE CAPTAIN with astonishment. "You're leaving the island?" they said in one voice, which they often did because they were twins and were always thinking the same thing.

"You can't leave the island!" Argo proclaimed. "Without you here we would be so . . . so . . ."

"Alone!" Arion completed Argo's sentence, as he often did.

"Arion is right!" Argo affirmed.

The Captain looked at the boys with kind eyes. "Just remember what I've taught you. And remember, I'll be back."

The boys couldn't imagine life on Terrene without the Captain. Argo and Arion were barely two years old the night their ship was wrecked and their parents were lost in the storm. The Captain and the boys drifted to this tiny island, made it their home, and named it Terrene. That was fourteen years ago. And now the Captain was leaving, and they felt afraid.

"There's so much more to life than Terrene. And when I return, we'll leave together—for Bluestone."

More to life than Terrene? As far as Argo and Arion knew, everything in the world was just like Terrene—small and gray. Not a happy gray like the hue of shadowed snow. Not a strong gray like the shade of thunderclouds. But a dirty, dismal gray—like the worn skin of an elephant or the cold ashes of a dead fire.

But if gray is all you've seen, gray is all you expect. "You've got to see with your heart—not your eyes," the Captain would challenge.

The Captain had spent many evenings sitting with the boys, explaining the grayness and the meaning of color. According to the Captain, long ago a volcano had erupted, burying forever the colors of the isle in a mountain of soot.

As a result, Terrene was a gray island in the middle of a big gray ocean. Waves with gray tips slapped against beaches with gray sand. Trees with gray trunks sheltered gray-winged birds. Gray animals with gray eyes would peer from behind the gray bushes.

Only the boys and the Captain were not gray.

A thick forest grew in the center of the island, and in the center of the forest there rose a mountain. The Captain told the boys to stay away from both.

He told them, "The volcano erupted once. It will erupt again."

"And stay out of the forest," he would say, "for the forest will take your color."

They believed the Captain because the Captain had seen a thousand islands. "There are islands," the Captain told them, "so vast you cannot walk around them even in two days!"

This amazed Argo and Arion, for they could run all the way around Terrene in one day.

"And there are islands where the sky is so clear and the water so sweet that the birds sing and the creatures leave the forest and come to the sand."

Amazing! Birds didn't sing on Terrene. And the creatures never left the forest.

"But there is one island that is most special."

"Bluestone!" the boys would state in unison. They knew the name well, for it was the Captain's home.

"Ahh, Bluestone," the Captain would smile. "There the birds always sing. Blue waters tumble over the shiny brown rocks, and the grass is ever green, and the sun sets on the horizon like an orange ball."

Argo and Arion would squeeze their eyes tight and try to picture the colors and hear the sounds. But they had never heard birds sing, and they'd only seen gray.

The Captain knew it was hard, so he would help them. "Look at each other," he would venture. "See your blue eyes? That is the color of water at Bluestone. And see your blond hair? On my island, there are birds and sunsets with such splendor. And your teeth, see how white? They are the color of Bluestone's sands. It's like nothing you've ever seen here in Terrene."

Then the Captain would grow very solemn. "Argo, Arion, you were not made for Terrene. You were not made to live in the gray."

Then his voice would grow soft with sorrow. "Terrene was like Bluestone once—alive with sights and sounds—long ago, before the volcano."

But his voice would be sad only for a moment. "Bluestone is not gray." His eyes would dance as he spoke. "And Bluestone is your true home."

"I am going away for just a short time," he said. "I'm going to Bluestone to prepare your place. But I will come back and take you there with me."

"But what do we do while you are gone?" they asked.

"Remind each other this is not your home. And help each other to be ready to leave when I return."

Though the boys believed the Captain, their hearts were sad as he climbed in his fishing boat and set sail for Bluestone. "I will return!" he shouted to them. "Be ready!"

So began the days when Argo and Arion were alone together on the island.

At first they were just alike and did exactly the same things. They would rise early in the morning, look at each other's faces, and think of Bluestone.

"Your eyes are like the waters we will see," one would say.

"And your hair is yellow like the birds we will hear," the other would answer.

"We were not made for Terrene," they would affirm. "We were made for another place."

Then they would spend their day together, dreaming of the Captain and remembering his words.

When the evening came they would go to the eastern beach from which he had sailed and recount his farewell. "I will return and take you with me," one would quote. "Be ready to leave when I return," the other would remind. And then they would rest for the night.

They spent many days searching the horizon for their Captain. Looking for his return was their greatest joy . . . at first.

But after many days Argo and Arion began to grow tired.

"It's hard for me to remember his voice," Argo confessed.

Arion added, "The colors are getting blurry."

One afternoon Arion had gone to sleep on the gray sand while Argo took his turn at the watch. When Arion awoke, Argo had left the beach. He didn't return until the evening sun was setting and Arion was already on the eastern coast.

"Where did you go?" Arion asked.

"I grew tired of the ocean and went into the forest."

"But the Captain said to stay out of the forest. We need to stay together, Argo—to watch."

Argo didn't respond. And that evening when the two boys retold the words of the Captain, Argo seemed uninterested.

When Arion awoke the next morning, Argo was gone again. Arion tried to see the colors and hear the music without the help of his brother, but it was hard. He felt alone, speaking into the sky with no one to listen, but he spoke anyway.

Several days passed before Arion saw his brother again. And when he did, Arion was shocked. He looked into Argo's eyes, longing to see the blue which would remind him of Bluestone, but the color was gone. Faded and pale was the hair which had been bright blond like the sun of the Captain's country.

"Argo, you've changed!"

"No, I haven't," Argo argued.

"What's happened?"

"I've made some new friends in the forest. The animals. They aren't evil. They've shown me things I've never seen before. We swim in the river and run in the meadow and crawl in the cave beneath the great mountain."

"Argo, have you forgotten the Captain's words? He said to stay away from the mountain. It could explode."

Argo laughed—a deep, husky laugh like the sounds which came from the forest late at night.

"The creatures have told me the truth, Arion. The volcano never exploded and it never will. That's just a fantasy. Come, I'll show you."

Arion looked at his brother for a long time. He looked at the eyes that used to sparkle and touched the hair that used to gleam. "You've changed, Argo. You are like the island."

"A little change doesn't hurt. Besides, what I'm doing in there is fun. Come with me."

"No, Argo, we must wait here. Maybe if you stay here, your color will return."

Argo laughed the dark laugh again. "Stay here and look for something that will never happen? And miss the fun of the forest? You're a fool, Arion. If the Captain was returning, he'd be back by now. Come on, let me introduce you to my friends."

"No, Argo. Stay with me and let me help you be ready for the Captain's return."

The two brothers stood and looked at each other—Arion with sorrow and Argo with disbelief.

"You really think he's coming, don't you? After all this time? If you'd seen what I'd seen in the forest, you wouldn't stay here on the beach."

Arion spoke firmly. "I've seen enough, Argo. The forest has taken your beauty. Stay with me. Change—before it's too late."

But Argo just smiled and walked toward the trees and became a part of the grayness.

Only a few days later a speck of gold appeared on the morning horizon—the color Argo's hair used to be, only a thousand times greater. It sparkled and beamed like a fire in the night. The light cut through the gray with splendor. It was a grand schooner with billowed sails of purest white.

The Captain had returned! Arion could see him on the bow of the ship.

"I am back!"

"I am ready!" Arion shouted as loudly as he could. The Captain waved.

When Arion boarded the ship, he raced into the Captain's arms. The weariness of the watch was forgotten. What Arion had been able to see only with his heart, he now saw with his eyes.

He thought of his brother and looked up at the Captain. "Argo chose Terrene."

Sadness came over the Captain's face. He walked to the rail and looked at the gray forest.

"Shall we go get him?" asked Arion.

"No, my child, he has made his choice."

And with that the ship set sail for Bluestone. Only when they reached the horizon did they feel the vibrations of the volcano.